PAPER CUTTING

Making all kinds of
Paper Shapes and Figures

by
ERIC HAWKESWORTH
illustrated by Margaret and Eric Hawkesworth

This book is
with grat
to
Eileen and To
Tom, Anne

S. G. Phillips ⚓ New York

Copyrig

Printed

Library of

TT870.H37

PAPER CUTTING

Making all kinds of
Paper Shapes and Figures

by
ERIC HAWKESWORTH

illustrated by Margaret and Eric Hawkesworth

S. G. Phillips ⚡ New York

Library of Congress Cataloging in Publication Data

Hawkesworth, Eric.
Paper cutting.

1. Paper work.   I.   Title.
TT870.H378   1977   736'.98   76-30461
ISBN 0-87599-224-2

23

Contents

8 *Contents*

Foreword

Paper cutting is a simple creative art requiring the minimum of skill and materials and all you need to make a start is paper, a pair of scissors and a pencil. All the basic types of paper folding are here described in detail together with methods of marking and cutting the folded packets to produce a wide variety of novel designs including a circle of swans and a chain of Humpty Dumptys falling down from a wall.

These basic folds are easily modified to extend the range of figures so that items such as three-dimensional models of a merry-go-round, a sentry box and a fort can be cut from folded paper bands while a giant beanstalk is produced from a special paper roll. At first, ordinary newspaper can be used to practice cutting the shapes and then all kinds of coloured papers can be added for extra effects.

The cut paper shapes can be used to illustrate stories and the book shows how sets of figures are linked together to plot the adventures of Jason and the Argonauts, the Pied Piper of Hamelin, the Three Little Pigs etc. One chapter recounts an exciting page of American history in a story about the Siege of the Alamo at San Antonio in Texas in the year 1836 in which the famous frontiersman Davy Crockett made his last stand. Paper cutting has many practical applications and, because the craft is well within the scope of young fingers, it is ideal for classroom projects. Strips of figures cut from plain white paper can be imaginatively painted by the children to make fine wall displays and the chapter showing how to make some original festive decorations using foils and coloured wrapping papers employs the basic techniques learned earlier in the book.

A set of programme notes is included to show how the craft of paper cutting can be used to present an interesting lecture-style entertainment.

If the dimensions of your local newspaper are not easily adapted to the directions, substitute large rolls of foolscap or brown wrapping paper. Be careful in handling the wrapping paper, however, as it can cause small but painful paper cuts.

Paper Cutting

Basic Paper Folds

Paper sheets can be folded in a variety of different ways in preparation for marking and cutting the many designs and this chapter teaches, with practical examples of original cut shapes and figures, some of the most important basic paper folds. Any kind of plain or coloured papers are suitable but, throughout the book, the use of ordinary newspaper sheets will be taken as a standard so as to convey more accurately the exact paper size to be used for each figure. Newspaper is ideal material to practise the folding and cutting and the page size of large double sheets is big enough to obtain most of the folds. All the sketches indicate, in step-by-step detail, how the paper strips and squares are folded, marked and then cut out to produce the illustrated designs.

FOLDING AND MARKING A LONG PAPER STRIP— SKULLS AND CROSSBONES

A large double newspaper sheet measuring, when fully opened out, approximately 32 inches (800 mm.) wide by 24 inches (600 mm.) high is refolded on its centre crease and then cut into two halves to produce two long paper strips measuring 32 inches (800 mm.) by 12 inches (300 mm.) as shown in the sketch. One of the strips is now folded, from your right to your left, three times with the first fold coming on the centre crease. Edges and ends of the paper strip must be kept square and in line while the creases are pressed in firmly. Next, the chosen design is marked out in half section with the folded edge of the packet to your right. The sketch shows a skull and

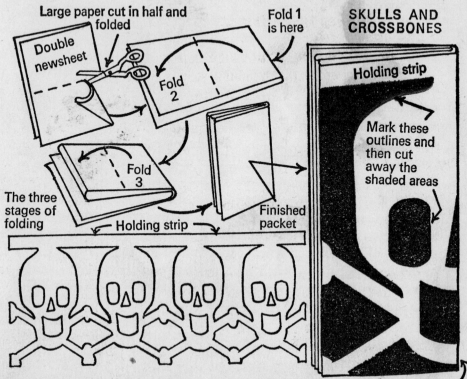

Large paper cut in half and folded

Double newsheet

Fold **1** is here

SKULLS AND CROSSBONES

Fold 2

Holding strip

Mark these outlines and then cut away the shaded areas

The three stages of folding

Fold 3

Holding strip

Finished packet

FOLDING AND MARKING A LONG PAPER STRIP

Folded edge

crossbone outline marked, as described, with the centre of the skull to the right-hand folded edge; by marking and cutting the figures in this way we are sure that, when the whole design is opened out, both sides of the shape are identical and indeed, the complete row of figures that the folded strip produces, will all look exactly alike. When marking out the skull and crossbones notice that a holding strip is incorporated in the figure at the top of the folded packet—this ties the row of four skulls together for easier display when the strip is fully opened. Copy the outlines as carefully as you can using a soft black lead pencil or crayon to go round all the contours. The nose and mouth openings are marked to the folded edge while the ends of the holding strip and the crossed bones are marked cleanly to the edge on the left-hand side of the packet. Eye socket holes are drawn as an elongated circle to complete the marking out. Use a sharp pair of scissors for the cutting and start snipping out the design by working along the holding strip and down the side of the skull—removing all the areas that are shown shaded in the diagrams. Trim away the paper sections to form the nose and mouth and finally cut out the eye. A safe method of starting the scissor point in central areas such as the eye socket is to double back the paper across the eye's centre line and then make a plain half-inch cut on this folded edge calculated to come somewhere near the middle of the area of paper to be cut out. The paper is then opened and the scissor point easily inserted for cutting out the hole. Using this method, even blunt-nosed scissors can be employed to produce quite intricate designs—so essential where young fingers are learning the craft. Display the finished cut figure by first unfolding the skull on its centre line and pressing the crease out flat. Now, grip the ends of the holding strip and open the row of skulls and crossbones out wide to reveal the string of identical figures. Of course, more than four figures can be produced if the initial paper strip is made longer to start with and examples of much longer strips are shown later in the book.

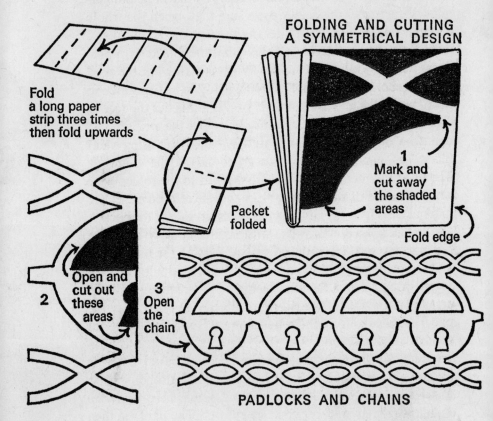

FOLDING AND CUTTING A SYMMETRICAL DESIGN

Fold a long paper strip three times then fold upwards

Packet folded

1 Mark and cut away the shaded areas

Fold edge

2 Open and cut out these areas

3 Open the chain

PADLOCKS AND CHAINS

FOLDING AND CUTTING A SYMMETRICAL DESIGN— PADLOCKS AND CHAINS

Another very useful basic paper fold is achieved when a long paper strip is given an extra fold on the horizontal centre line of the packet to produce designs that are symmetrical top and bottom. First, fold a long paper strip three times right to left —exactly like the strip used for the skull and crossbones figure—and then fold the packet upwards one more time as shown in the sketch. Mark the chain design as before using a black pencil and then cut round the outlines cleanly. Unfold the cut packet one fold and you will see that we have a figure with identical chains top and bottom with a circular disc shape in between. To turn these discs into padlocks two further cuts have to be made and the drawing shows how the keyhole and clasp are marked and then cut away to the folded edge of the packet. Open the finished design by pressing out the centre crease to make the padlocks lie flat, then grip the ends of the upper chain and extend the whole set of padlocks and chains. It is surprising how quickly quite intricate shapes and patterns can be cut from this type of fold and later chapters explain how more than one figure can be produced from the same symmetrical fold using just a few simple cuts.

FOLDING A VERTICAL PAPER STRIP—A CHAIN OF HUMPTY DUMPTYS

Instead of cutting figures to appear as a long row, paper strips can be folded vertically so that finished designs unfold in a sort of chain. Clowns, monkeys and acrobats look particularly effective when cut from this type of strip because the miniature figures make an unexpected appearance hanging hand to hand and feet to feet in a living chain. An ideal size

FOLDING A VERTICAL PAPER STRIP

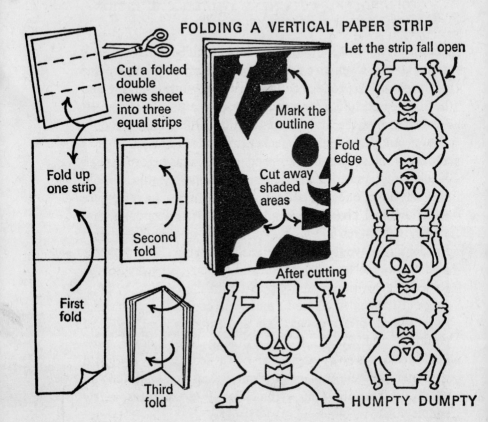

Cut a folded double news sheet into three equal strips

Fold up one strip

First fold

Second fold

Third fold

Mark the outline

Cut away shaded areas

Fold edge

After cutting

Let the strip fall open

HUMPTY DUMPTY

for these paper strips is 32 inches (800 mm.) long by 8 inches (200 mm.) wide and they are easily cut from double news-paper sheets—each double sheet producing three such strips as shown in the sketch. Prepare a strip by folding it up twice and then making a third fold *across* the packet and pressing all the creases flat. With the fold-edge of the packet to your right, mark the outline of Humpty Dumpty as given taking care to bring the top of the hat, hands and feet to the upper and lower edges of the folded packet. Nose, mouth and bow are marked to the folded edge and the eye needs to be cut as an egg-shaped hole. Cut away all the surplus areas and remove the eye section, then you can open the middle fold and press the figure of Humpty Dumpty out flat. You turn the figure into a sort of animated cartoon as you tell the story of Humpty Dumpty and then show how he fell off the wall. Grip the upper ends of the strip and let all the figures fall and unfold—the sketch shows how the chain of paper Humpty Dumptys appears with each hanging on to the other.

CUTTING FROM A SQUARE SHEET—A POOL OF SWANS

Many interesting designs can be cut from a square sheet of paper—tablecloth patterns, wheels and other sets of figures in a circular format—and the paper is prepared by laying out a large double news sheet and then cutting off one of the sides to produce a square measuring 24 inches each way. An easy way of ensuring an exact square is shown in the sketch; the sheet is folded across from one end diagonally and firmly creased when the top edges of the paper are level. Then the surplus strip is cut away flush to the folded sheet, leaving you with a perfect square. Lay the sheet out flat in front of you and make the first fold upwards as you double the sheet in half. The second fold is made from your left to your right—form-ing the packet into quarters—and then a third fold is made corner to corner on the diagonal crease that will be showing

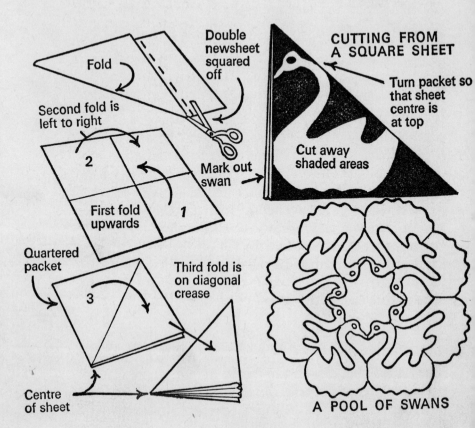

Fold

Double
newsheet
squared
off

Second fold is
left to right

2

1

First fold
upwards

Mark out
swan

Quartered
packet

3

Third fold is
on diagonal
crease

Centre
of sheet

**CUTTING FROM
A SQUARE SHEET**

Turn packet so
that sheet
centre is
at top

Cut away
shaded areas

A POOL OF SWANS

from when the sheet was originally squared. Turn the packet
so that the centre of the folded sheet is at the top and then
mark out the swan motif, copying the outlines that are given
in the sketch. Notice how the beak and back of the neck are
carried right to the edge of the folded packet as well as the
base of the neck and the swan's tail so that the finished birds
are all joined together at these points in the pattern. Draw a
fancy wavy line across the bottom of the swan to represent
water—this gives the opened-out circular design an attractive
serrated edge. Carefully cut round the outlines and remove
the eye detail by doubling back the paper across the swan's
head and snipping a small semi-circular segment from the
fold. Show the cut design in three stages—first display a single
bird, then open out a second swan. Finally, shake out and
show the complete pool of swans. This way of folding a
square sheet produces a set of eight motifs in circular fashion;
by giving the packet extra folds during the preparation we
can add other effects such as the one described in the next
type of fold.

A SQUARE SHEET WITH EXTRA FOLDS—SPIDER IN THE TREE

Make up another square paper sheet and fold it as just
described up to the quartered packet stage and then make
two more folds as shown in the sketch. The first fold is made
left to right on the diagonal corner-to-corner crease and then
the paper is folded back to the diagonal fold-edge to produce
the triangular-shaped packet ready for marking. Pencil the
outlines as indicated by the shaded areas in the drawing—a
series of slots and ribs—and then cut the pattern out cleanly.
You can now open the design two folds and show a tree shape
by holding it with the trunk stem at the bottom. This paper
cutting design is really a surprise item because by making two
more small cuts the tree can be fully opened to show a large

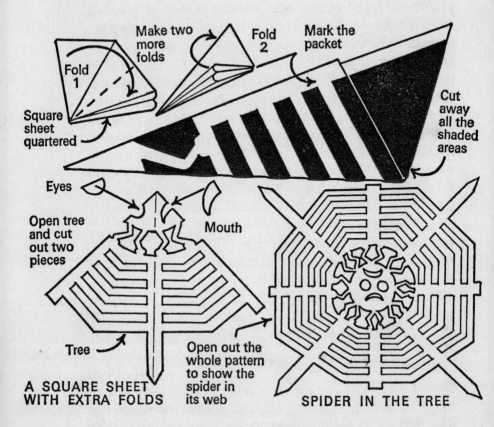

Make two more folds

Fold 2

Mark the packet

Fold 1

Square sheet quartered

Cut away all the shaded areas

Eyes

Open tree and cut out two pieces

Mouth

Tree

Open out the whole pattern to show the spider in its web

A SQUARE SHEET WITH EXTRA FOLDS

SPIDER IN THE TREE

spider's web ... with a spider in the middle! After showing the tree for a few moments a small semi-circle and a curved segment are cut from the tip of the tree pattern in the positions indicated and then you can shake out the whole design. The spider appears as a many-legged creature in the middle of his web and can be shown either way up because his eyes and mouth are a symmetrical design and look the same whichever way it is viewed. When paper cutting is presented as an entertainment this type of dual figure is of great value in keeping an audience surprised and interested and, because such designs are easily developed from one figure to the next, help to keep a story plot flowing.

CUTTING FROM A PAPER BAND—A MERRY-GO-ROUND

An interesting development of folding the papers is achieved by gluing paper strips into bands *before* folding and cutting, to produce novel three-dimensional models; the example given here constructs a rabbit merry-go-round with base platform and shaped canopy. In the story routines that follow later in the book the same technique is employed to make a sentry box complete with toy soldiers and a model fort. Choose a thickish piece of newspaper for this figure—some newspapers may have thicker paper than others or try wrapping paper—and cut a strip measuring 24 inches (600 mm.) by 10 inches (250 mm.). Form the strip into a band and glue right down the overlapped joint. Press the band flat and then make two folds from right to left to make a packet 3 inches (75 mm.) wide by 10 inches (250 mm.) high as shown. Place the packet in front of you with its folded edge to your right and pencil the half-section rabbit design as shown in the sketch on to the paper making sure that the centre of the rabbit is on the folded edge. Cut neatly round the outlines starting with the canopy and working down to the base and clip out a diamond-shaped eye by folding the paper back across the

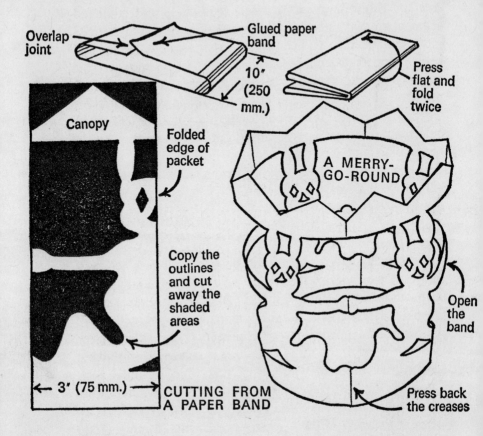

Overlap joint

Glued paper band

10″ (250 mm.)

Press flat and fold twice

Canopy

Folded edge of packet

A MERRY-GO-ROUND

Copy the outlines and cut away the shaded areas

Open the band

← 3″ (75 mm.) →

CUTTING FROM A PAPER BAND

Press back the creases

head as already described for some of the other figures. Open the cut paper band and press out all the creases so that the figure will stand up on its own, having the appearance of a model roundabout. Coloured drawing papers could be used in classroom to create miniature fairground displays—other simple shapes such as clowns and dolls are easily adapted into the design—and the thicker papers would enable children to crayon or poster-paint the merry-go-rounds in flamboyant fairground style.

MAKING A LADDER FROM A ROLL

Tubes rolled up from paper are cut and shaped to provide some very surprising productions because the nature of this type of basic fold allows for quick opening into figures that are quite unexpected. A tree and a giant beanstalk are featured in other stories in the book—each figure employs a different sized strip to obtain the right effect—but the method of rolling the paper tubes is exactly the same as that to be described for the construction of a long paper ladder. Four single newspaper sheets each measuring 24 inches (600 mm.) long by 16 inches (400 mm.) wide are glued end to end, taking care to run a continuous glue line down each joint as shown. When dry, the paper strip is rolled up from one end into a tube of about $1\frac{1}{2}$ inches ($37\frac{1}{2}$ mm.) diameter—if the strip is laid out on a long table and the roll is started carefully it is easy to complete the rolling by pushing the tube along with the palms of your hands. Glue the end of the paper lightly to prevent the tube unrolling. Mark out for the ladder construction by dividing the tube into three parts and making firm pencil lines in two places nearly across the width of the tube. The sketch shows how these two lines are terminated $\frac{1}{2}$ inch (12 mm.) from the edge of the tube and then a third line is drawn between the other two—rather like the crossbar of the letter H. Make cuts through the thickness of the tube along the outer

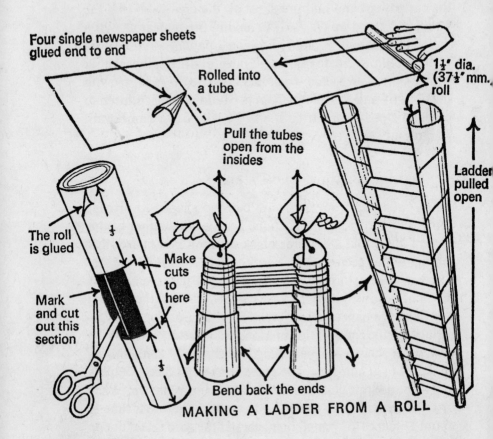

Four single newspaper sheets glued end to end

Rolled into a tube

1½" dia. (37½" mm.) roll

Pull the tubes open from the insides

Ladder pulled open

The roll is glued

⅓

Make cuts to here

Mark and cut out this section

⅓

Bend back the ends

MAKING A LADDER FROM A ROLL

lines and then snip along the crossbar removing the surplus paper as shown by the shaded area in the drawing. Open the ladder by bending back the tube ends and pulling up the tubes by gripping the *inside* coils of the paper. As soon as the ladder starts opening you can shake out all the rungs as you expand the figure to a height of at least 4 feet (1,200 mm.). As the opened ladder is self supporting it can lean against a chair or table—a useful method when the item is being included in a story routine—or it can be taped to a wall for a more static display.

OTHER TYPES OF FOLDING

The basic paper folds just described can be altered and adapted to suit different designs and page sizes like the twin giants in the Jack and the Beanstalk story that are made by simply folding a large double news sheet twice before marking out. A set of fighting skeletons that Jason encounters in his quest for the Golden Fleece are made to rise out of the ground because you have *pleated* a double-length paper strip for easy opening. A figure that is a combination of the long vertical paper strip and a paper band produces a chain of climbing Jacks that are given animated motion by revolving them over your hands. There are designs that conceal other figures such as the dragon that opens to reveal a bow and arrow—and opens still further to make a compass; Mr. Wolf in the Three Little Pigs can be shown as a three-dimensional figure but when the paper is opened he has vanished into the flower beds! And Brer Fox changes into Brer Rabbit and his family when the paper strip is simply turned upside down. Some basic origami folds are used to turn a sheet of check pattern wrapping paper into a magic kilt; when shapes that resemble snowballs, skis and a woolly hat are cut from the kilt the paper is shaken open to show that it has turned into a snowman! All sorts of colour effects become possible when coloured papers are used in place of the newspaper sheets that are recommended for practice and a chapter explains the creation of some original festive decorations.

STORIES CUT FROM PAPER

Paper cutting can be made both instructive and entertaining with the addition of simple story plots that link together a few suitable designs and figures, and if the papers are folded and marked out before the demonstration the presenter can tell his story as he cuts each shape. Using items already described in this chapter one could tell how a pirate's treasure map turned into a row of skulls and crossbones . . . and how the buried treasure was secured with a set of padlocks and chains! The treasure chest was hidden in a lagoon that was shaped like a swan . . . and guarded by a ring of ghostly swans! Many folk had tried to find the treasure by pacing off the distance from a tree on the shore of the lagoon . . . but all were thwarted by the man-eating spider that lived in the tree! Using the other figures one could recount how Humpty Dumpty fell off the merry-go-round at the fair and couldn't get on again . . . until the fairground owner came along with his long ladder! The craft offers great possibilities for illustrating all kinds of stories. In the following chapters the author has suggested basic patter outlines to go with each plot but extra dialogue should be added to suit the presenter's individual style.

The Pied Piper of Hamelin

All the figures needed to illustrate the famous tale of the Pied Piper's visit to Hamelin are made from a single long paper strip. First, the paper is rolled into a tube to represent the magic flute and then the tube is cut in half and the two shorter tube sections are used to cut out long strips of rats and the children of Hamelin. This is another example of a different type of paper fold because instead of having to fold or pleat a paper strip to produce a row of figures a rolled paper tube is simply flattened and marked with the half-section shapes prior to cutting them out.

PREPARING THE PAPER FOLD

A double news sheet is cut in half to obtain a strip measuring 12 inches (300 mm.) wide by 32 inches (800 mm.) long and this is rolled into a tube of about 1 inch (25 mm.) diameter and the roll is secured by fitting a rubber band at each end as shown. If you wish to mark out the figures before telling the story then the tube needs to be lightly flattened so that the end of the rolled strip is level with one side of the tube. Draw a line across the centre of the tube and then mark the rats on one side and the children on the other, remembering to leave holding strips at the top of each set of figures. The drawing shows how the figures are marked in exactly the same way as folded or pleated packets so that the finished shapes are produced all joined together. Press the tube back to its cylindrical form and you are ready to present the routine.

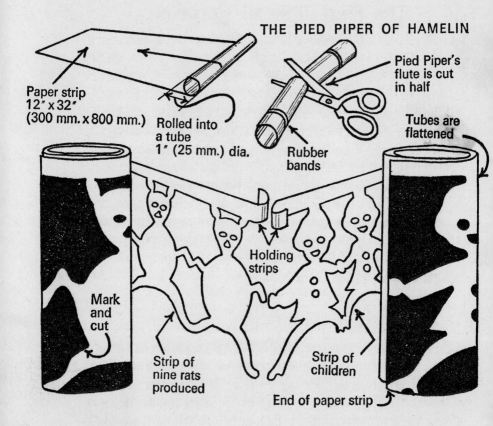

THE PIED PIPER OF HAMELIN

Paper strip
12″ x 32″
(300 mm. x 800 mm.)

Rolled into
a tube
1″ (25 mm.) dia.

Pied Piper's
flute is cut
in half

Rubber
bands

Tubes are
flattened

Mark
and
cut

Holding
strips

Strip of
nine rats
produced

Strip of
children

End of paper strip

PRESENTING THE STORY: WHAT TO SAY AND DO

'Everyone remembers the story of Hamelin, a mediaeval town in Germany standing on the banks of the River Weser, and how the people were plagued with rats. Robert Browning's poem tells how the rats were everywhere . . . in babies' cots and even in old men's hats! The citizens were desperate and the mayor and his corporation offered huge sums of money to anyone who could rid the town of the rats. A stranger—dressed in a suit of red and yellow—offered to help, claiming he possessed a magic charm . . . a flute, exactly like this paper tube . . . and with it he could lure the rats into the river!'

Show the paper roll and hold it up to your lips with fingers set along the tube—then mime the action of playing a flute or recorder. Pick up your scissors and cut the tube in half—the rubber bands will prevent the paper unrolling. Start cutting out the rats while you continue the story:

'The mayor offered the Pied Piper one thousand guilders if he could keep his promise . . . soon, the colourful stranger was walking down the main street of Hamelin . . . playing a merry jig on his magic flute. The rats came tumbling out of the houses as they heard the music . . . and followed him in a squeaking procession, out through the town gates and down to the river. And this is how they all looked as they scurried to their doom!'

Open the strip of rats by gripping the end of the rolled figures and letting the paper unfurl. The securing rubber band is removed once cutting has started on the flattened tube. Hold and display the string of rats for a few moments—there should be nine of them if the tube is originally rolled to the 1 inch (25 mm.) diameter—and then ask someone to hold the figures while you make a start on the second strip. Where several cut figures are being used to tell a story such as this it makes a very effective display if people are invited to hold the designs as they are produced. Again, remove the rubber band and flatten the tube as you cut out the children of Hamelin.

'But once the town was rid of its rats, the mayor went back on his promise to pay the Pied Piper his one thousand guilders . . . he offered the Piper only fifty guilders! In great rage, the Pied Piper took up his magic flute and played a different tune . . . and this time all the children of the town followed him along the streets! In a great laughing column they trailed the Piper's heels as he led them to a hillside beyond the town. A cavern opened in the side of the hill . . . and the children disappeared inside . . . for ever! Watch all the children go!'

Unroll and display the strip of children, then tear off the end child as you explain:

'Only one small boy lived to tell the tale about the Pied Piper of Hamelin . . . because he was lame he had trailed behind the others and had seen the mountain close on all his friends. It taught him never to break a promise!'

Jason and the Golden Fleece

Jason sets sail in the good ship Argo in his quest for the Golden Fleece and the first cut paper illustration depicts this young hero prince with three of his friends—the Argonauts. Many perilous adventures befall them and they have to defeat the strange creatures, half-human, half-bird that are called the Harpies, before they reach Colchis, land of the Golden Fleece. The goddess Juno comes to Jason's aid when the King of Colchis sets Jason the impossible task of slaying an army of fighting skeletons that arise from a crop of dragon's teeth— she makes Medea, the King's daughter, fall in love with Jason by shooting Cupid's arrow through her heart, and Medea uses her magic charms to help Jason capture the Golden Fleece. Novel paper designs and figures are used to highlight all the main points of the classic tale and the final shape is expanded from Cupid's bow and arrow to produce Juno's compass that guided the Argonauts back safely to Thessaly.

PREPARING THE PAPER FOLDS

All the five folds needed for this story are made from large double newspaper sheets and most of them are slight modifications of the basic methods of folding already described.

JASON AND THE ARGONAUTS

Instead of cutting the double news sheet in half to produce a row of four figures the whole page size is used as shown in the sketch. Fold the double pages on the centre crease, then make

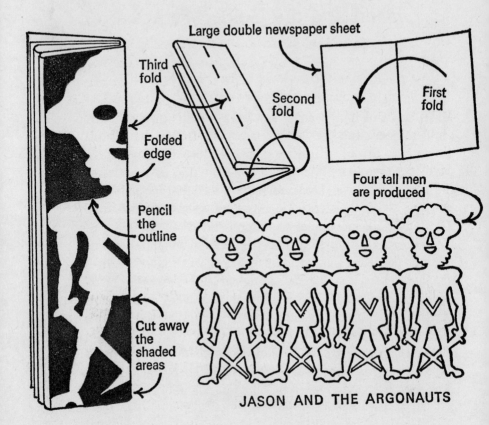

Large double newspaper sheet

Third fold

Second fold

First fold

Folded edge

Four tall men are produced

Pencil the outline

Cut away the shaded areas

JASON AND THE ARGONAUTS

two further folds from your right to your left—keeping the edges nice and level and pressing in all the creases firmly—to form a finished packet 4 inches (100 mm.) wide by 24 inches (600 mm.) long. Lay the packet with the folded edge to your right and pencil mark the outline of Jason holding his sword, as given. Notice how the sword blade is marked with the tip bent at right angles to the blade—this produces a set of crossed swords in the finished figures. The nose, mouth and V-shaped belt are marked to the folded edge and the eyes are ovals. No holding strip is needed with this figure because the heads are joined together at the hair line to give sufficient support to the row of Argonauts. Other points of contact between the four tall men are at the shoulders and toes.

THE THREE HARPIES

A long paper strip measuring 24 inches (600 mm.) by 12 inches (300 mm.) is folded into three equal sections by turning each end of the strip inwards, and then this packet is given another fold to form the centre line for marking out the three Harpies. As before, lay the packet with the folded edge on the right and copy the Harpie drawing as accurately as you can. Points to watch are the horn tips which are cut at right angles —like Jason's sword—to give a crossed horn effect in the completed figures, and the wing tips which are joined to the side of the head as shown. The mouth section is shaped like a letter H and this produces grinning fangs when the paper is opened (p. 36).

THE GOLDEN FLEECE

Trim the edge off another double sheet to make it square and then fold the paper into quarters. This quartered packet is now folded twice more—turning the ends in as indicated to divide the packet into three equal sections. This type of fold

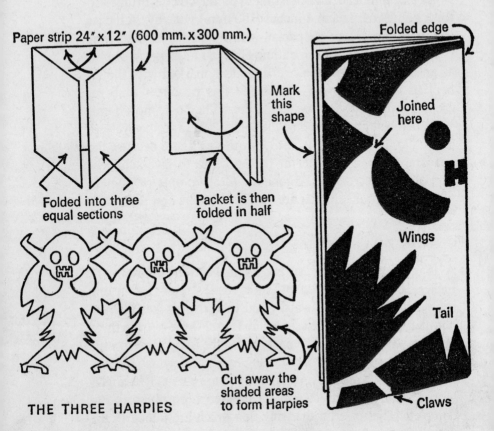

Paper strip 24" x 12" (600 mm. x 300 mm.)

Folded into three equal sections

Packet is then folded in half

Mark this shape

Folded edge

Joined here

Wings

Tail

Claws

Cut away the shaded areas to form Harpies

THE THREE HARPIES

gives you six motifs round the edge of the finished design. Mark the rams' heads, noting how the horn tips are joined to the sides of the heads and how the eyes are drawn as pear shapes. Small diamond patterns are snipped away from the middle of the design to suggest the Golden Fleece (p. 38).

THE FIGHTING SKELETONS

Cut a double news sheet in half to obtain two standard long paper strips and then glue the two pieces together. Mark pencil lines along the strip at 4-inch (100 mm.) spacings and use these lines as guides to *pleat* the double-length paper. Lay the packet with the upper and lower free ends of the pleated strip to your left—as shown—and mark the skeletons to the right-hand fold-edge. Again, we do not need the plain holding strip across the top of the design because the crossed swords of the fighting skeletons give adequate support when the figures are pulled open: it is important to join the sword tips to the tops of the heads when you are drawing and cutting this design (p. 40).

THREE FIGURES FROM ONE DESIGN

This fold is prepared from another paper square, folded into quarters and then folded twice more—once on the diagonal centre line and then folded back to bring the edges to the middle as for the Spider in the Tree in the first chapter on basic folds. The dragon outline is copied carefully to obtain feathered wings and tail, and the eye is drawn as a $\frac{1}{2}$-inch (12$\frac{1}{2}$-mm.) circle. After cutting, this figure is first shown as a dragon by opening the head spikes and twisting the tail. Then the paper is opened just one fold to reveal Cupid's bow and arrow, and finally the whole design is opened and shaken out to form Juno's compass. Prepare the story ready for showing by laying out all the paper folds—fully marked and ready for cutting—on your table in the order that they will be used—

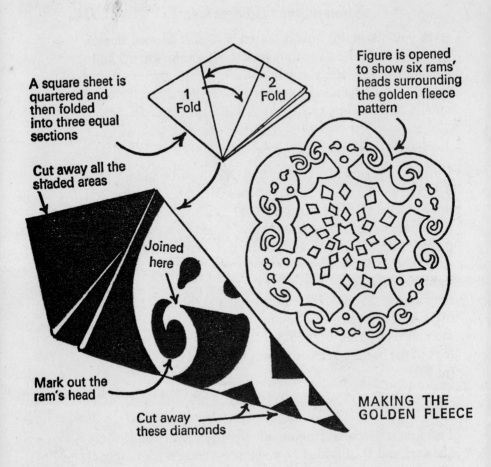

A square sheet is quartered and then folded into three equal sections

1 Fold

2 Fold

Figure is opened to show six rams' heads surrounding the golden fleece pattern

Cut away all the shaded areas

Joined here

Mark out the ram's head

Cut away these diamonds

MAKING THE GOLDEN FLEECE

with Jason on top. Have your scissors to hand together with a waste-paper basket for disposing all the cut pieces tidily (p. 42).

PRESENTING THE STORY: WHAT TO SAY AND DO

'Jason's quest for the Golden Fleece is a classic adventure story of Greek mythology . . . it tells how Jason's uncle, King Pelias of Thessaly, sent the young prince on a dangerous mission to a faraway island, hoping the quest would be fatal, because when Jason became of age he would wear the crown. Jason set sail in a ship called the Argo . . . with a crew that included Hercules, Theseus and the Sons of the North Wind . . . here we see Jason with three of his Argonauts . . . standing on the prow of the ship with their swords drawn and crossed . . . ready to take on any monster that might rise from the deep!'

Cut cleanly round the outlines removing all the surplus areas that are shown shaded in the drawings. Press out the centre fold and show just one completed figure, then pull the strip out fully to display Jason and the Argonauts—all the men are 24 inches (600 mm.) tall because the fold was constructed from a whole double sheet. Let someone hold the figure while you pick up the strip that is marked for the Harpies. Open the strip out wide to show your audience, then refold and start cutting as you continue the story:

'The Argonauts' first port of call was a tiny island that had just one human inhabitant . . . a blind old man who had the power of seeing into the future. The great god Jupiter had punished the old man for his gift of second sight by sending three winged creatures called Harpies to snatch his food . . . they had claws . . . and horns . . . and evil fangs, like this!'

Point out the various features of the design as you cut round the outlines—it all helps to keep your audience interested—then open out the three bird-like figures after pressing out the centre crease in the usual way. The drawing shows

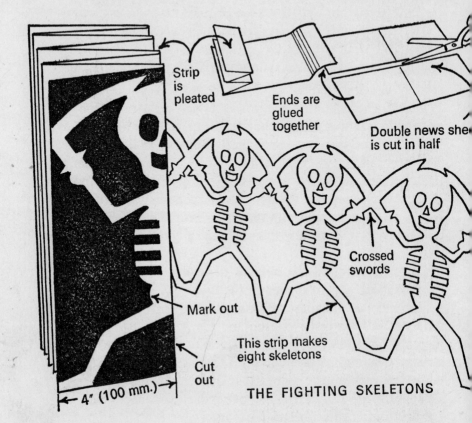

Strip is pleated

Ends are glued together

Double news sheet is cut in half

Crossed swords

Mark out

Cut out

← 4" (100 mm.) →

This strip makes eight skeletons

THE FIGHTING SKELETONS

how they appear with opened wings, crossed horns and gaping fangs.

'Jason and his men drove the Harpies away for good and the old man was go grateful that he looked into the future and described all the dangers that lay ahead for the Argonauts . . . and how to avoid them! After many weeks' sailing, the ship reached Colchis and Jason demanded the Golden Fleece from the King. This is how the fleece looked . . . a dazzling golden thread sheepskin . . . surrounded by six rams' heads!'

The Golden Fleece pattern is easy to cut out but care should be taken to shape the eye correctly and also to remove that section of paper *within* the rams' horns so as to leave a connecting piece on to the head. If we do not tie the designs together properly the finished figures will flop and be hard to display. This is particularly important in circular designs where half of the figures are upside down. The author uses a sheet of gold metallic foil paper for this figure with brilliant effect when the Golden Fleece is opened—an example of what can be achieved once the presenter has become used to cutting designs from newspaper.

'The King of Colchis agreed that Jason could take the Fleece . . . providing he could first accomplish a seemingly impossible task. The young prince had to sow a crop of dragons' teeth from which would grow an army of fighting skeletons! Jason then had to fight and defeat them all . . . single-handed!'

Show the pleated paper without revealing the nature of its folding or its extra length and start the cutting at the top of the strip. Work round the main outline—arms, body and legs— and cut away the larger areas of surplus paper first. Then the smaller details can be removed such as the eyes, nose and mouth and the rib bones snipped out as shown. Finally, the section of paper inside the sword arm is cut away, leaving the sword tip joined to the top of the skull. Open the cut packet by laying it on a chair and then lifting the pleats as you show how the skeleton army grew out of the ground.

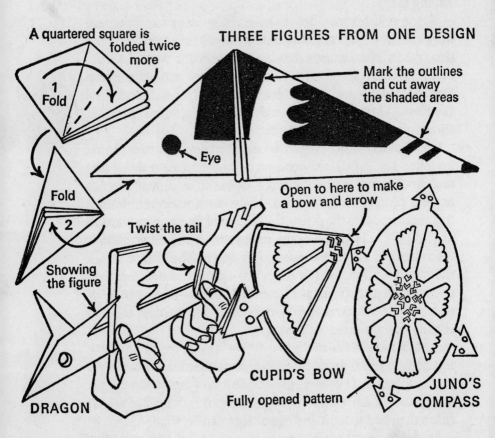

A quartered square is folded twice more

1 Fold

Fold

2

Showing the figure

THREE FIGURES FROM ONE DESIGN

Mark the outlines and cut away the shaded areas

Eye

Twist the tail

Open to here to make a bow and arrow

DRAGON

CUPID'S BOW

Fully opened pattern

JUNO'S COMPASS

'When Jason saw the skeleton army arise . . . like this! . . . he was dismayed . . . but the goddess Juno came to his aid and gave him magic powers to slay the entire troop . . . in a very short time the battlefield was a mass of broken bones! But the King of Colchis still refused to give Jason the Golden Fleece . . . and so Juno used her powers of magical persuasion again! The Golden Fleece was guarded by a dragon . . . so let me show you how to cut out a dragon from another sheet of folded paper!'

Pick up the final paper fold and cut away for the head, wings and tail. Double back the paper across the head and snip out a semi-circle to form the eye disc. You show the dragon by holding the figure at the base of its wings between the left thumb and first finger after opening the paper points above the head to form a pair of horns. The right hand twists the tail of the figure through a complete turn and secures the roll between finger and thumb—as shown in the sketch.

'The King's daughter was called Medea and Juno made her fall in love with Jason . . . by shooting Cupid's arrow through her heart . . . with a bow and arrow that looked like this!'

Unfold the dragon design along its centre crease and show the bow and arrow formation. Hold the figure in the same manner that you would bend and aim a real bow and arrow—with one hand holding the paper bow and the other fingers clipped round the tail feathers of the arrow.

'Medea told Jason a magic charm to lull the guardian dragon to sleep and soon they had taken the Golden Fleece back to the Argo and were steering home to Thessaly. The Argonauts had many more adventures on the return journey . . . but Juno's compass guided them through all the dangers. Here is Juno's compass . . . appearing like magic when we open out the bow and arrow!'

Shake open and display the compass with its four cardinal points projecting as shown in the drawing.

The Adventures of Brer Rabbit

Here is another example of a two-in-one design that is developed from a long paper strip but in this instance the figures are made reversible so that the second set of characters is revealed when the paper strip is turned upside down. Brer Fox and Brer Wolf go calling on Brer Rabbit and his family and decide to eat the young ones when they find Brer Rabbit absent. But Brer Rabbit returns in time and outwits the Fox and the Wolf with a trick involving a jar of treacle! After cutting and showing Brer Fox and Brer Wolf the presenter holds the two of them by their heels as he opens out the strip to reveal Brer Rabbit and all his family!

PREPARING THE PAPER FOLD

Cut and fold a long paper strip in the usual way for making a row of four figures—identical to the Skulls and Crossbones fold in the first chapter—and then mark out the design given in the sketch. A holding strip is needed across the top of the packet from which to hang the Fox and the Wolf by their ears, and two sets of eyes and mouths are marked and cut in the positions indicated. The upper paw and tip of the lower foot are drawn across to the left-hand edge of the folded packet to form connecting points for the strip of figures.

PRESENTING THE STORY: WHAT TO SAY AND DO

'Brer Fox and Brer Wolf were not really the best of friends—neither trusted the other!—but on this particular day the two

THE ADVENTURES OF BRER RABBIT

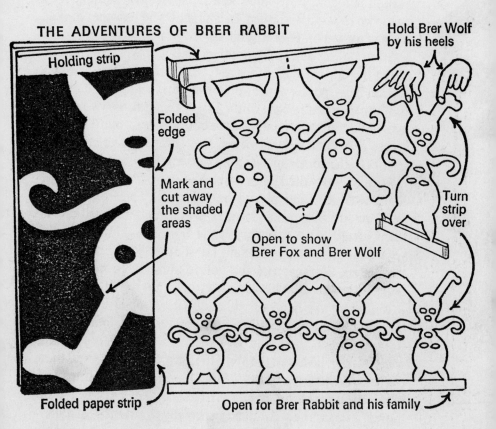

Holding strip

Hold Brer Wolf by his heels

Folded edge

Mark and cut away the shaded areas

Open to show Brer Fox and Brer Wolf

Turn strip over

Folded paper strip

Open for Brer Rabbit and his family

of them went calling on Brer Rabbit and his family. Brer Rabbit had gone out somewhere . . . so the Fox and the Wolf sat down to await his return. Let me show you how they looked as they waited on Brer Rabbit's front porch.'

Start cutting along the holding strip and work round and along the upper edge of the front paw. Snip out the other big section between the upper and lower paws and then shape the bottom leg and the base of the body. Clip out the two sets of eyes and mouths to complete the cutting. Press out the centre crease and show just the one figure first which you name as Brer Fox, then open out a second shape and call him Brer Wolf.

'While they waited, Brer Rabbit's young family of fat little bunnies frisked and played on the lawn. The Fox and the Wolf made a plan . . . as soon as Brer Rabbit returned one of them would keep him busy while the other kidnapped the young rabbits! Brer Wolf said he would talk to Brer Rabbit and let the Fox capture the young bunnies, so he went to meet Brer Rabbit, who was carrying a big jug of molasses.

Refold the two figures so that only Brer Wolf is showing and illustrate how he jigged down the road to meet Brer Rabbit.

'Now Brer Rabbit was very wise and he knew something was amiss . . . he asked the Wolf to taste the molasses and then told him it was fox's blood. "Fox's blood!" replied Brer Wolf liking the sweet taste greatly. "I know where I can get some more!" . . . and he went racing off ready to eat up Brer Fox!'

Turn the strip upside down and hold the figure by its heels —with the holding strip at the bottom. Open the strip out wide showing the four rabbits in a row as you conclude the story:

'While Brer Wolf was hot on Brer Fox's heels, chasing him all over the countryside, Brer Rabbit gathered all his little bunnies together and they sat and laughed . . . and laughed . . . and laughed . . . just like this! Brer Rabbit explained that the poor old fox didn't know if he was on his head . . . or his heels!'

Jack and the Beanstalk

Figures for this story include a giant beanstalk rising magically from a special paper roll and a chain of climbing Jacks that are made to move by rolling them over your hands. A pair of giants nearly 3 feet (900 mm.) long are produced from a double newspaper sheet folded vertically— they first appear as smaller figures but are made to grow to their full height by unpinning a special fold. Jack climbs the beanstalk and steals the magic harp from the giants. This harp changes into an axe enabling Jack to chop down the beanstalk and kill the giant who is clambering down in pursuit. Finally, the axe changes into Jack's star of fortune—providing wealth and happiness for the lad and his mother.

PREPARING THE PAPER FOLDS

Newspaper is used again to make the folds but, as the presenter gains experience, other types of coloured papers may be gradually introduced into the story. Gold foil paper turns the magic harp into a golden instrument, for instance.

MAKING THE BEANSTALK

Five single newspaper sheets are glued end to end to form a long paper strip and then this is rolled into a tube of about $1\frac{1}{2}$ inches ($37\frac{1}{2}$ mm.) diameter—as described in detail for the construction of a paper ladder in the first chapter dealing with basic methods of folding. Glue the end of the strip to the side of the completed tube and then mark the tube end ready for

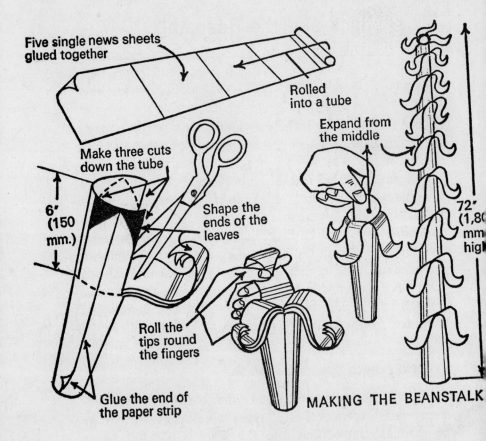

Five single news sheets glued together

Rolled into a tube

Make three cuts down the tube

6″ (150 mm.)

Shape the ends of the leaves

Expand from the middle

72″ (1,8 mm. hig

Roll the tips round the fingers

Glue the end of the paper strip

MAKING THE BEANSTALK

cutting during the story. Make three pencil marks down the sides of the roll—equally spaced and to a depth of 6 inches (150 mm.) as shown in the sketch. After cutting, these strips are bent outwards to form the beanstalk's foliage but first, their tips need to be rounded off to provide a more realistic shaping. Pencil the rounded tips as indicated to make the cutting sure and easy while you are telling the story. After a few repeat demonstrations of any of the paper folds the presenter will find it possible to memorise the shapes without much marking out in advance.

JACK CLIMBS THE BEANSTALK

Two paper strips each measuring 24 inches (600 mm.) long by 6 inches (150 mm.) wide are glued into a continuous band using small overlapped joints, care being taken to spread the glue along the joint in an unbroken strip. Press the band flat, then make two folds up from the bottom as shown, pressing the creases in firmly. The third and final fold is made from right to left across the packet to form a centre fold for the figures. Keep this final fold-edge to your right, then mark out the half shape of Jack by copying the drawing. Notice how the hands and feet of the character are taken to the top and bottom edges of the packet. Eyes, mouth and buttons are drawn in ready for cutting during the story (p. 50).

THE TWIN GIANTS

Open out a large double news sheet and lay it with its narrow edge towards you. Fold it in half from your right to your left across its vertical centre line—as shown—and then make a second fold in the same direction. This gives you a folded packet that is 32 inches (800 mm.) long by 6 inches (150 mm.) wide. Draw a guide line across the middle—12 inches (300 mm.) from the top—then make a folded pleat 4 inches

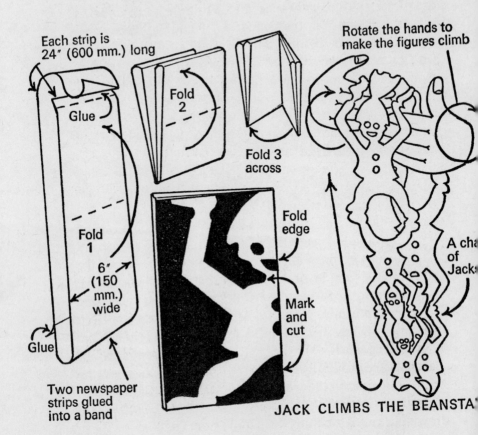

Each strip is 24" (600 mm.) long

Glue

Fold 1

6" (150 mm.) wide

Glue

Two newspaper strips glued into a band

Fold 2

Fold 3 across

Fold edge

Mark and cut

Rotate the hands to make the figures climb

A cha of Jack

JACK CLIMBS THE BEANSTA

(100 mm.) deep in the bottom half of the packet, letting the top of the pleat come level with the half-way guide line across the strip. Push a long straight pin through the folded packet to secure the pleat. Next, mark out the figure of the giant holding his mallet head-high—the mallets are connected to the hair—and the body is spaced so that the bottom of the jacket is level with the top of the extra pleat. The legs are drawn over the pleated section as shown and the giant's foot is sketched in at the bottom of the unpleated section of the packet. After the figure has been cut out in the usual way the pin can be extracted to make the giant grow taller in a most surprising manner. The twin characters produced represent the giant and his wife (p. 52).

THREE MORE FIGURES FOR JACK

This design is a triple production from one paper fold which is made from a square sheet like the Spider in the Tree figure described in the chapter on basic folds. After quartering the square sheet, it is folded twice more diagonally to make the triangular-shaped packet. The axe outline is very easy to draw and, after the figure has been cut out during the story, it can be shown in three different ways. First, it is opened one fold to show the magic harp, then it is refolded to make the axe and finally it is opened completely to form the wheel-shaped star of fortune. The figures are presented in this sequence to match the story line. Lay out the marked papers in the order to be used—beanstalk, climbing Jacks, twin giants and, at the bottom, the triple production (p. 54).

PRESENTING THE STORY: WHAT TO SAY AND DO

'Jack and the Beanstalk is an often-told tale, but here is another way of telling the story . . . with illustrations cut from ordinary newspaper! When Jack's mother sent the lad to

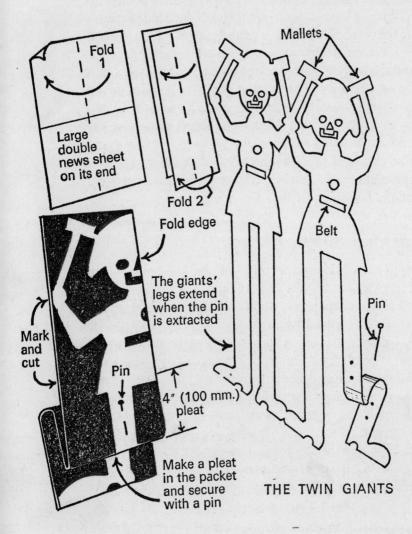

Fold 1

Large double news sheet on its end

Fold 2

Fold edge

Mallets

The giants' legs extend when the pin is extracted

Belt

Mark and cut

Pin

Pin

4" (100 mm.) pleat

Make a pleat in the packet and secure with a pin

THE TWIN GIANTS

market to sell their cow called Milky White she little expected her son would bring home in return just five small beans! Of course Jack tried to explain to his mother that they were magic beans . . . but she threw them out of the window in anger.'

Pick up the beanstalk tube and make the three cuts through the wall of the roll. Shape the ends of the leaves, then bend the three cut sections outwards as shown. Roll the tips of the leaves round your fingers to make them curl, then you are ready to expand the figure. Grip the inner coil of the paper roll and lift and extend the beanstalk from its middle. Expand and shake open the beanstalk till it is 6 feet (1800 mm.) high— the five-sheet roll from which it is constructed enables you to stretch open the figure quite safely. Lean the beanstalk against a chair or table as you say:

'But by next morning the beans had taken root and the beanstalk had risen to a great height . . . its topmost foliage was hidden from view amid the clouds! Jack decided to go and seek his fortune by climbing the beanstalk . . . let me show you how to cut out the brave lad from this folded piece of paper! This is his head . . . and his arms . . . and his coat! You wouldn't believe it but these semi-circles of paper are the buttons from Jack's jacket!'

Cut round the outlines and remove the smaller details, then press out the centre crease and display a single figure. Open out the continuous band and show a chain of Jacks joined together—like the vertical strip of Humpty Dumptys in the first chapter—by their hands and feet. Place your hands inside the band of figures, with the backs of the hands towards the audience, and give movement to the little men by rotating the hands to make the chain of Jack's climb. During the story Jack goes up and down the beanstalk several times and this can be simulated—up or down—depending on which direction you turn your hands.

'Here we see Jack climbing the beanstalk . . . hand over

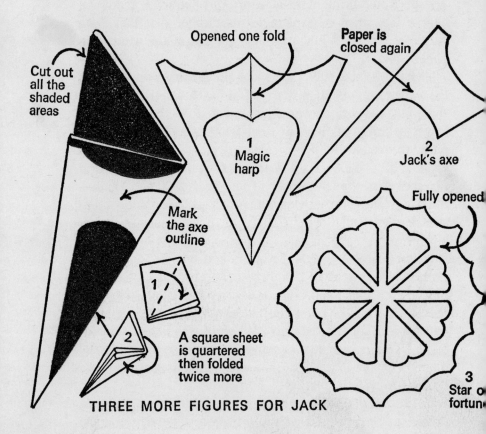

Cut out all the shaded areas

Opened one fold

Paper is closed again

1 Magic harp

2 Jack's axe

Mark the axe outline

Fully opened

A square sheet is quartered then folded twice more

3 Star o fortun

THREE MORE FIGURES FOR JACK

hand! . . . and when he reached the top a long white road stretched out before him. At the end of that road stood a huge castle . . . home of a couple of giants . . . the husband and his wife! Jack stole a bag of gold and a hen that laid golden eggs and took them back to earth . . . his arms grew tired climbing up and down the beanstalk . . . like this! But he returned for the third time to see what else he could capture from the giants.'

After cutting out the giants, hold up and show the packet with the pleated leg still pinned up. Remove the pin and let the legs open to twice their original length, then open and display the twin giant figures.

'Jack had only seen the giants when they were sitting down . . . and it came as a shock to see how tall they really were when they stood up on their long legs! They were a fearsome sight as they chased Jack round the castle . . . brandishing their mallets!'

Ask someone to hold the twin giants while you start cutting the axe shape out of the fourth paper fold. This is quite a high-speed production because only two cuts are needed to remove all the surplus areas. Do not reveal the axe shape to the audience at first but open and show the magic harp figure at this point in the story.

'Jack hastened towards the castle door . . . pausing just long enough to pick up a magic singing harp that stood in the hall. The harp began calling for its master . . . "Help! . . . Help!" it cried as Jack ran as fast as he could back to the top of the beanstalk. The road shook as the giant pounded after the lad . . . but soon Jack had reached earth and he called to his mother to fetch an axe!'

Close the harp shape together to form the axe, then demonstrate how Jack chopped down the beanstalk. Hold the beanstalk with one hand and make chopping motions with the paper axe. Then let the beanstalk topple over on to the floor.

'With a few mighty blows from the axe, Jack severed the

beanstalk, making it crash to the ground . . . with the giant still clinging to the foliage! Everyone came from miles around to see the magic singing harp which turned out to be Jack's lucky star of fortune. If we open the magic harp . . . like this . . . you will see the symbol of the lad's good fortune!'

Unfold the harp and display the fully-opened figure as the star of fortune. At the end of any paper cutting story always ask your audience if anyone would like to keep the paper productions as a little souvenir of the entertainment. The figures can be carefully refolded into their creases and even items such as the ladder or the beanstalk can be reclosed into something like their original form.

Going to St. Ives

This is another example of a symmetrical paper fold that opens to make a variety of figures and with it we can tell the story about going to St. Ives. Only two simple cuts are needed and then the paper can be shown as a number seven, a letter M, a bow and a mask and finally, when the strip is fully opened, the audience see a row of four Xs . . . representing four wrong answers to the question of how many were going to St. Ives.

PREPARING THE PAPER FOLD

A standard long paper strip—cut from a large double news sheet to measure 32 inches (800 mm.) by 12 inches (300 mm.)—is folded right to left three times and then given an extra upwards fold as shown in the sketch. With the fold-edge to your right, mark the figure as a backwards number seven and then the packet is all ready for cutting.

PRESENTING THE STORY: WHAT TO SAY AND DO

'I remember my old school teacher posing us the problem about how many were going to St. Ives . . . I'm sure you all know the poem . . .

> *As I was going to St. Ives,*
> *I met a man with seven wives;*
> *Each wife had seven sacks,*
> *Each sack had seven cats,*

GOING TO ST. IVES

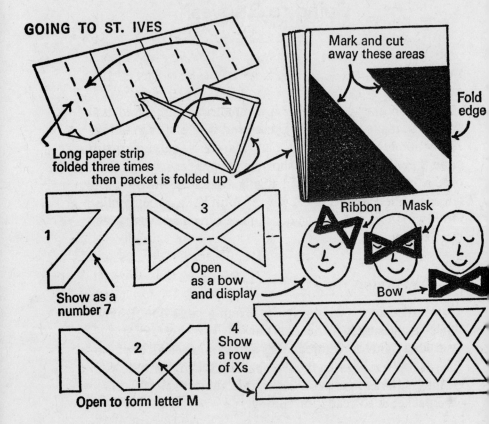

Long paper strip folded three times then packet is folded up

Mark and cut away these areas

Fold edge

1 Show as a number 7

3 Open as a bow and display

Ribbon   Mask

Bow →

2 Open to form letter M

4 Show a row of Xs

Each cat had seven kits;
Kits, cats, sacks and wives,
How many were going to St. Ives?

Pick up the packet and cut out the two shaded areas to form the number seven . . . it will appear the right way to the audience out front if you hold it in front of you as drawn.

'Our teacher explained that it would help us to understand the problem more easily if he presented it in a visual fashion . . . so he cut out the number seven from a folded sheet of paper . . . this being the number of kits, cats, sacks and wives on the road to St. Ives. And to remind us of the question the teacher then went on to unfold the paper . . . converting the number seven into a letter M . . . M standing for how *many* were going to St. Ives.'

Unfold the number seven symbol along its centre crease and present the next figure as a letter M by turning the packet on its side as shown in the sketch. After showing for a few moments open the letter M figure one fold of the paper to convert the shape into a figure that looks like a bow tie. This shape is now used to mime some of the characters in the poem—it is held against the head to represent a ribbon bow for the wives and used as a mask when the cats are mentioned. Move the figure down in front of your neck to illustrate how the kittens had bows about their necks. Make the changes smoothly and pause long enough to let the audience appreciate each character mime as they are made.

'Each wife had a ribbon in her hair . . . like this! . . . and the cats are represented by a mask over their eyes. The teacher said we would remember the kittens easily if we thought of them wearing bows round their necks! So that was the problem . . . how many were really going to St. Ives?'

The paper is opened still further to show a pair of Xs—just keep unfolding the paper strip in the reverse order to which it was originally folded up. Explain as you display this figure:

'Harry Smith said there were 21 going to St. Ives . . . and my friend Fletcher had a guess at 49. Both were wrong answers . . . this is how our teacher marked their copy books . . . with a couple of crosses for their trouble! I rather thought the correct total might be 28 and Brown, the brains of the class, worked out the astronomical total of 2,401 . . . what a crowded road to St. Ives!'

Pull out the paper strip fully to display the row of four Xs as you conclude the story:

'Of course . . . we were all wrong . . . look at this row of crosses! Only one was going to St. Ives! Our teacher explained . . . to have *met* all these characters on the road implied that they were all *coming from* St. Ives, therefore only the writer of the poem was actually journeying to that town!'

Three Little Pigs

The three little pigs and their houses are cut from standard three-fold paper strips but Mr. Wolf is developed by folding a paper square in a different fashion. After cutting, Mr. Wolf can be shown in two ways, full face and profile, depending on how the paper is unfolded, but when the pigs look for the wolf inside the paper all they can find is a flowerbed design. When the sheet is refolded, out pops Mr. Wolf again!

PREPARING THE PAPER FOLDS
THE THREE LITTLE PIGS

A sheet of newspaper measuring 12 inches (300 mm.) by 24 inches (600 mm.) is folded into three equal parts by turning in each end of the strip. To obtain accurate folds draw two pencil guide lines down the paper strip at 8-inch (200-mm.) spacings and use these lines as the fold points. Press the creases in firmly, then make one more fold from right to left to form the centre of the design. Mark out the half shape for the pigs, as shown, noticing that a holding strip across the top is needed for displaying the figures. The pigs' feet are drawn across to the left-hand edge of the packet and each figure is provided with a curly tail.

THREE PIGS' HOUSES

These are marked on an identically folded paper strip as for the previous figure. The sketch shows how the houses are joined together at the base of the walls and at the roof line. The two

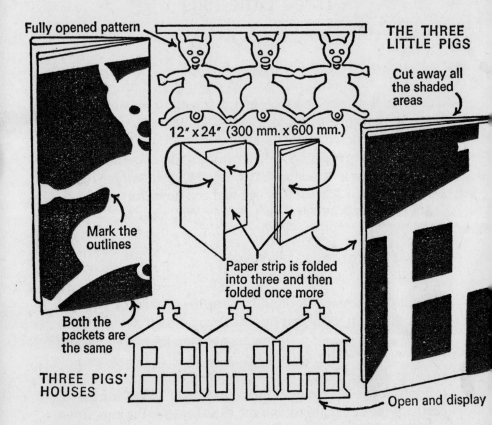

Fully opened pattern

THE THREE LITTLE PIGS

Cut away all the shaded areas

12″ x 24″ (300 mm. x 600 mm.)

Mark the outlines

Paper strip is folded into three and then folded once more

Both the packets are the same

THREE PIGS' HOUSES

Open and display

windows are simple rectangles and the door is cut to the centre-fold edge. No holding strip is needed with this figure.

MR. WOLF IN THE FLOWERBED

A newspaper sheet measuring 24 inches (600 mm.) square is folded in half and then, with the fold-edge towards you, each side is folded diagonally in to meet in the middle as shown. Make another fold from each side and then close the packet together to produce the triangular-shaped packet for marking out. There are five small areas to cut out in this design and they are pencilled in the positions indicated on the sketch; these produce a design that is different in principle from most of the other figures in the book because while all the other shapes are formed by what is called relief cutting—removing surplus paper *between* the characters so that the figures themselves stand out in bold relief—the flowerbed pattern is produced by a series of holes in a solid paper background. Place the three folded and marked papers on your table and you are ready to tell the story (p. 64).

PRESENTING THE STORY: WHAT TO SAY AND DO

'Here is the tale of the three little pigs . . . three fat little pigs that ate so much their mother sent them away to look after themselves. You will see how chubby they looked after I've cut them out of this paper strip . . . ears, snout and feet . . . and we must not forget their little curly tails!'

You can unfold the first paper strip and let your audience see that it is just an ordinary newspaper piece, then refold the strip ready to start cutting. Because the initial preparation of the papers is such an important part of the paper cutting art it adds greatly to a demonstration to let everyone see how at least one basic type of fold is put together during any single story presentation. Cut round the outlines and remove the

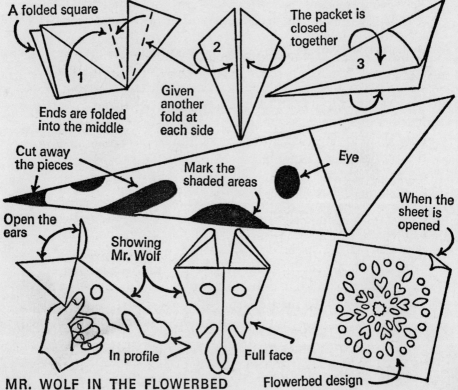

A folded square

Ends are folded into the middle

1

Given another fold at each side

2

The packet is closed together

3

Cut away the pieces

Mark the shaded areas

Eye

When the sheet is opened

Open the ears

Showing Mr. Wolf

In profile

Full face

Flowerbed design

MR. WOLF IN THE FLOWERBED

snout, mouth and hollow section of the tail from the folded-edge crease. Open and display the figure, then make a start on the second paper fold.

'The story tells how the little pigs built three houses . . . one of straw, one of wood and one of bricks . . . so our next illustration will be of these three houses. All the buildings had chimneys . . . and windows . . . and a door, which was essential to keep out Mr. Wolf! This is how the row of houses looked when all the work was completed. But Mr. Wolf had been watching all the time from his lair amid the flowerbeds . . . just across the road!'

Children love to come on stage and hold the figures as they are produced and by this point in the story you can have the pigs on display at one side of the platform and the strip of three houses on the other. Start cutting Mr. Wolf by snipping out the eye disc and removing the other sections as drawn. Bend back the two paper points and show Mr. Wolf in profile —the sketch shows how the figure is displayed by holding between the left-hand first finger and thumb.

'Mr. Wolf visited the first house and asked to come in . . . but when the first little pig refused the wolf huffed and puffed . . . till the house of straw fell down! He went to the next house . . . and pressed his face up against the window . . . like this!'

Open the paper fold along its centre crease and show Mr. Wolf full face. Tell how he blew the house of wood down when the second little pig refused to let him in. Next shake open the whole sheet and show the flower design.

'All three little pigs hurried to the house of bricks and looked out of their window . . . but Mr. Wolf had returned to the flowerbed and had disappeared into his secret lair! . . . he was nowhere to be seen!'

Refold the paper and produce Mr. Wolf in profile once more. Walk across to the row of houses that your assistant is holding and blow hard on the strip as you demonstrate how the wolf returned at night to try and blow down the house of bricks.

'But the house was too strong for Mr. Wolf ... so he climbed on to the roof and slid down the chimney! The pigs were waiting ... with a big kettle of boiling water! Mr. Wolf went yelping out of the house ... just like a scalded cat! ... and vanished for good in the flowerbed!'

Open the sheet and show the flowerbed design for a climax to the story.

The Magic Kilt

This is the story of a small Scots boy playing at winter games; when he wears his family tartan kilt he believes he cannot be beaten. The kilt is cut and folded from a sheet of patterned wrapping paper of a suitable check design and, as the presenter tells the story, different shapes are cut from the kilt. These shapes represent some of the junior highland games—skiing, throwing the snowball and knocking the snowman's hat off—and a surprising finish is reached when the kilt is shaken open to reveal a giant snowman! The cut-away sections of snowballs, ski and ski hat form the eyes, mouth, nose and buttons for the figure.

PREPARING THE PAPER FOLD

Choose a standard size sheet of tartan or check pattern wrapping paper measuring approximately 20 inches (500 mm.) wide by 28 inches (700 mm.) long, then fold it in half longways with the pattern showing to the outside. Next, with the centre fold to your right, mark out with pencil the outline of the snowman. The sketch shows how the head and body are proportioned by marking a line 12 inches (300 mm.) from the top of the sheet and making this the shoulder line of the snowman. Cut out the shape cleanly, then make a crease diagonally from the shoulder line as indicated. To disguise the snowman shape the paper is folded to represent a kilt and this is done by laying the sheet out flat with the white side uppermost and then making three folds. The first fold gathers together the head, which is then folded down on the two diagonal creases;

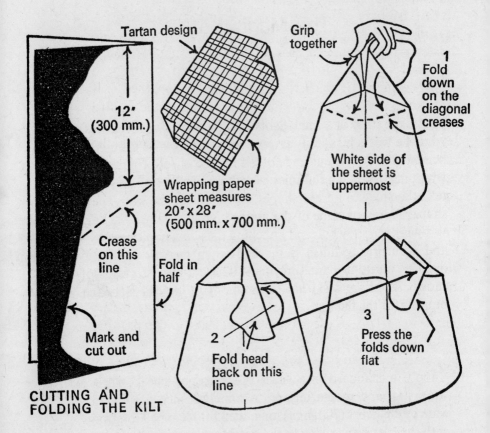

Tartan design

12"
(300 mm.)

Wrapping paper
sheet measures
20" x 28"
(500 mm. x 700 mm.)

Crease
on this
line

Fold in
half

Mark and
cut out

Grip
together

1
Fold
down
on the
diagonal
creases

White side of
the sheet is
uppermost

2
Fold head
back on this
line

3
Press the
folds down
flat

CUTTING AND FOLDING THE KILT

the second fold is made across the snowman's head level with his ears and finally, the head is pressed down flat on the right-hand side of the paper so that the folded portion is level with the sloping edge of the kilt shape. Turn the folded paper round so that the tartan pattern is showing and you are ready to present the story. The drawing which shows how the kilt is turned into a snowman indicates the positions of the various cut-out pieces and these may be lightly pencilled beforehand. The eyes are drawn as half-circles on the folded head and the nose and mouth are marked on the centre line. The two large buttons down the front of the snowman are also drawn as semi-circles (p. 70).

PRESENTING THE STORY: WHAT TO SAY AND DO

'Jamie McTavish was a young Scots lad who lived high above the snowline on the side of a mountain. Naturally, he became very good at winter games . . . he had to ski down to the school in the village every day . . . and so you can imagine how thrilled he was to hear he'd been invited to represent his school in the junior winter games. This is Jamie's kilt . . . and the lad was so proud of his tartan that he believed while he wore it no one could beat him in any of the events!'

Show the paper kilt, keeping the special folds to the rear, and then pick up the scissors and cut away the eye discs from the folded-down head. Because of the way the paper is folded only one half-circle of paper needs cutting away to produce a pair of paper discs which are shown to the audience with their white sides forward. These are described as snowballs.

'The first game was called throwing the snowball . . . each lad had two balls to try and gain the greatest distance. Here are the snowballs that Jamie threw! . . . of course the lad won hands down!'

The paper is now unfolded along the eye crease and the two sections representing the nose and mouth of the snowman are

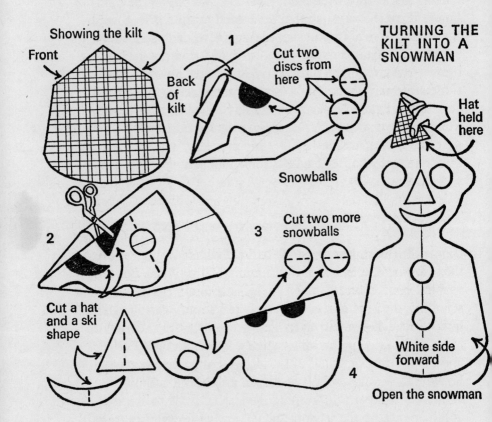

Showing the kilt

Front

Back of kilt

1 Cut two discs from here

Snowballs

TURNING THE KILT INTO A SNOWMAN

Hat held here

2

Cut a hat and a ski shape

3 Cut two more snowballs

4

White side forward

Open the snowman

cut out next. The drawing shows each stage of cutting with areas that are to be removed shaded in. The triangular-shaped nose is presented as a hat and the mouth is turned into a ski.

'Skiing down the side of a mountain was another exciting game . . . here is one of Jamie's skis! . . . and again, the lad was first past the winning post! The best game of all was knocking the snowman's hat off . . . this paper shape represents a woolly tartan ski hat and all the contestants had to throw more snow-balls at a giant snowman that was wearing the hat!'

Unfold the head completely and make the two final cuts on the centre line of the body—removing the snowman's button discs as shown. Display these as another pair of snowballs. Shake open the snowman and present him with the white side of the paper to the front as you say:

'It was Jamie who knocked the snowman's hat off and if we open the paper kilt you will see the big snowman . . . without his hat! At the end of the day Jamie was declared the junior champion . . . and the snowman got his hat back again!'

Finish off the story by holding the paper ski hat—tartan side forward—to the top of the snowman's head.

THE ALAMO FORTRESS

Paper strip

Measures 32" x 7"
(800 mm. x 175 mm.)
Cut away
the shaded
areas

First fold

Glued into a
band then
folded flat
twice more

Second fold

8" (200 mm.)
square

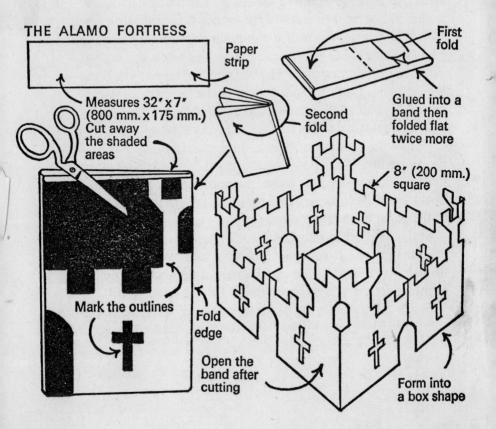

Mark the outlines

Fold edge

Open the
band after
cutting

Form into
a box shape

Siege of the Alamo

The famous siege of the Alamo which took place at San Antonio in Texas during the year 1836 is retold using cut paper illustrations and the story recounts how a handful of volunteer soldiers—including Colonel Jim Bowie and Davy Crockett—held the fort for nearly two weeks against the might of a 4,000-strong Mexican army led by their General Santa Anna. A model of the Alamo fortress is cut from a folded paper band and the defending volunteers are represented by a row of four frontiersmen who are produced wearing cowboy costume. The Mexicans attack with rope ladders but are repelled, so they decide to lay siege till the main troops arrive. Four soldiers in a model sentry box stand guard—this is another figure cut from a paper band—and then a row of eight soldiers are produced to depict the full-strength army. They attack the Alamo again and again but the brave volunteers are not vanquished until a cannon fires a hole through the walls. A paper cannon wheel symbolizes their heroic resistance that led to Texan independence.

PREPARING THE PAPER FOLDS

Sheet sizes and methods of folding for some of the figures in this story differ from the basic folds but should present no difficulty if the instructions are followed carefully.

THE ALAMO FORTRESS

A paper strip measuring 32 inches (800 mm.) long by 7 inches

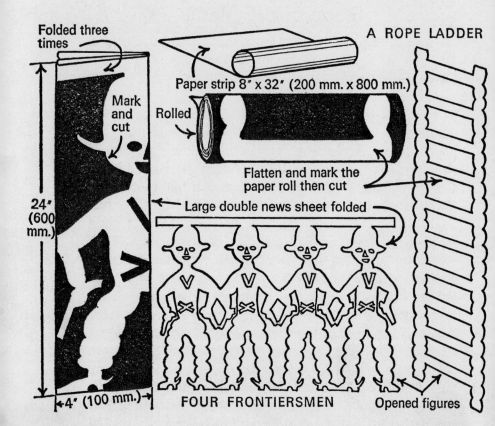

Folded three times

Mark and cut

24" (600 mm.)

←4" (100 mm.)→

A ROPE LADDER

Paper strip 8" x 32" (200 mm. x 800 mm.)

Rolled

Flatten and mark the paper roll then cut

Large double news sheet folded

FOUR FRONTIERSMEN

Opened figures

(175 mm.) wide is glued into a continuous band using a small overlapping joint that has a line of glue all the way down. Press the band flat, then make two more folds from right to left as shown in the sketch. Place the folded edge to your right and mark the outlines of the fort with its corner towers, doors and wall openings in the positions given.

FOUR FRONTIERSMEN

The sheet for this figure is folded up like a long paper strip but the whole double news sheet is used—like the construction for Jason and the Argonauts—so that after folding the strip three times in the usual way you finish up with a packet measuring 24 inches (600 mm.) high by 4 inches (100 mm.) wide. The cowboys are pencilled to a centre line on the right-hand fold-edge and there is a holding strip across the top joining to their stetson hats. Details on these figures include pistols, leg chaps, spurs and crossed gun-belts.

A ROPE LADDER

This figure makes a ladder that is different from the expanding tube construction described in the chapter on making basic folds. A paper strip measuring 8 inches (200 mm.) wide by 32 inches (800 mm.) long is rolled into an inch-diameter tube and secured with an elastic band. Flatten the tube slightly, then mark out the shape shown in the sketch. Notice how the ends are contoured so that the finished, opened ladder looks as though it is made from thick rope.

MAKING A SENTRY BOX

Use a sheet of paper measuring 10 inches (250 mm.) high by 24 inches (600 mm.) long and glue the ends into a band formation as shown. Flatten the band and then fold it twice from

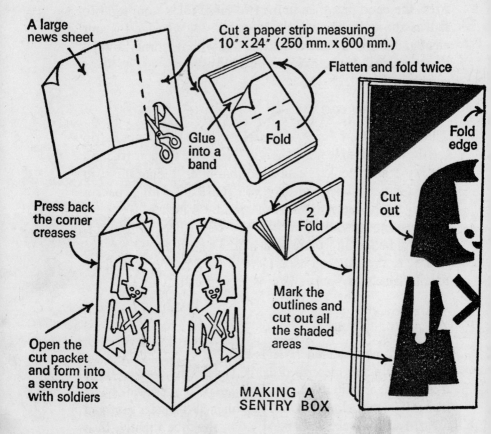

A large news sheet

Cut a paper strip measuring 10" x 24" (250 mm. x 600 mm.)

Flatten and fold twice

Glue into a band

1 Fold

Fold edge

Cut out

Press back the corner creases

2 Fold

Open the cut packet and form into a sentry box with soldiers

Mark the outlines and cut out all the shaded areas

MAKING A SENTRY BOX

the right-hand side leaving the fold-edge on your right.

Mark the sentry box outline—it is just a single-cut sloping roof—and then copy the soldier standing in the doorway. The sketch has the areas which are to be removed shaded in, and you will see that there are only two such main sections to be cut out. Draw in the eyes, mouth and crossed belts to complete the marking out.

EIGHT MEXICAN SOLDIERS

A standard long paper strip—used to make rows of four figures in most of the other stories—is given an extra fold before marking the characters, giving you a packet that is 12 inches (300 mm.) high by 2 inches (50 mm.) wide. Pencil the centre line of the soldiers to the fold-edge and notice that there are joining strips both top and bottom of the packet. Because of the extra fold eight figures will be produced in the finished cut strip (p. 78).

CANNON WHEEL

This is formed by folding a square sheet in the basic fashion—first into quarters and then twice more diagonally to make the triangular-shaped packet. Draw the cannon wheel markings as shown with the wheel spoke down the centre of the packet. The outer rim of the wheel needs to be drawn as a curved line to give the finished figure a circular outline. This completes the set of six prepared papers that are needed to tell the story and they are placed on the table with your scissors. Have a waste-paper basket to hand for disposing of all the cut pieces (p. 78).

PRESENTING THE STORY: WHAT TO SAY AND DO

'Davy Crockett is one of the folk-lore heroes of the USA and his adventures are told in song and story . . . but few people

EIGHT MEXICAN SOLDIERS

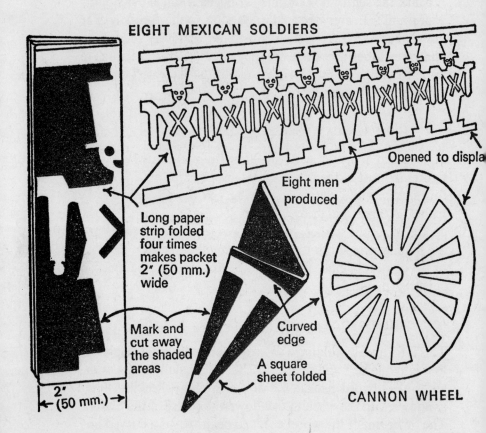

Opened to displa

Eight men produced

Long paper strip folded four times makes packet 2″ (50 mm.) wide

Curved edge

A square sheet folded

Mark and cut away the shaded areas

2″ (50 mm.)

CANNON WHEEL

know of his gallant last stand in the famous siege of the Alamo
... defending his homeland during the Texas War of Independence in 1836. Davy, with a handful of other volunteer soldiers
who were mostly cowboys, fortified an old mission building
called the Alamo near San Antonio ... and waited for the
Mexican troops to attack across the river Rio Grande.'

While you make this introduction to the story you can
start cutting out the first figure which is the Alamo fortress.
Make clean cuts into the corners of the battlements and snip
out the windows, wall and door openings. When the cutting is
complete the band is unfolded and formed into a square by
pressing out some of the creases so that the figure will stand
four-square as shown in the sketch. Stand the fortress on the
table, then make a start cutting out the four frontiersmen.

'Here is a model of the Alamo fortress ... inside its walls
waited the cowboys and frontiersmen under the command of
Colonel Bill Travis ... knowing that they alone had to face
the invading army until Sam Houston in the north could
raise an army to defend Texas!'

The four frontiersmen will appear from the cut paper strip,
as illustrated, holding their guns at the ready as they stand
shoulder to shoulder, suspended from the holding strip across
the top of their stetsons. You will see that the four characters
are joined together at elbows, gun tips and boot toes to keep
them all in a line.

'Another of the men was named Jim Bowie ... better
known as the inventor of the famous Bowie knife. They presented a determined line-up as they stood behind the battlements of the fort ... with guns loaded and drawn! Frontiersmen all ... from their ten-gallon stetsons down to their riding
boots and spurs!'

The frontiersmen can be displayed by hanging them over
the front edge of the table—pin or clip them to a dark tablecloth for the best effect—then the tube for making the rope
ladder figure can be started. Remove the rubber band when

you start the cutting and then allow the ladder to unroll naturally by holding the ends as the paper falls under its own weight.

'The vanguard of the Mexican troops appeared and immediately attacked the Alamo with rope ladders ... hoping to scale the walls and take the men by surprise. But the cowboy sharpshooters were too good for the attackers ... the rattle of Colt ·45s sent the Mexicans scurrying for cover in the cottonwood grove. The general of the attacking army was named Santa Anna and he decided to lay siege to the fortress until his main troops—4,000-strong!—arrived. Here is a sentry box ... cut from another band of paper ... containing four of the guards!'

Some of the detail-cutting round the guardsmen in the sentry box needs care and should not be hurried. Their eyes, mouth and cross straps across the tunics are cut to the right-hand fold-edge as shown. Open the cut packet and form the box into a square by re-creasing some of the corners. Stand the sentry box by the side of the model fort on the table, then proceed with the cutting of the eight Mexican soldiers. The design of these figures is similar to the guards in the sentry box but much taller of course; their cutting out follows a like pattern. Open and extend the finished strip at the point mentioned in the story.

'For twelve days and nights the brave defenders of the Alamo stood fast against all attacks ... but all the while General Santa Anna was building up his great army. Every hour saw the arrival of a new company across the plain from Mexico ... they must have looked a fearsome sight to the men in the fort! Here is another squad of eight Mexican soldiers marching on the Alamo!'

Cut out the cannon wheel figure and open it as you continue:

'Santa Anna warned he would take no prisoners when he finally attacked ... but the men of the Alamo refused to surrender! The Mexicans brought up cannons and breeched the fortress walls . . . this represents one of the cannon wheels. In the last battle the Alamo finally fell . . . but the stubborn resistance of Davy Crockett and his colleagues had bought enough time to enable the Texans to raise an army under Sam Houston to chase Santa Anna all the way back to Mexico. The Alamo still stands today . . . symbol of Texan freedom!'

A MONTAGE OF THE SCENE

All the cut paper figures could be assembled on a display board to build a picture of the siege for a classroom project. You would need to open the fort into a long strip for a central feature and the sentry box could be cut into four pieces for fixing to each corner of the display. The other figures would be attached according to scale height with the taller items in the foreground. Items from other stories could also be added, such as the paper ladder from the first chapter.

Billy Goats Gruff and the Troll

The three Billy Goats Gruff go trip trapping over the bridge until they are stopped by the Troll. Each goat sends his bigger brother in turn to face the Troll and it is the eldest goat that finally butts the Troll into the river to clear the way to the greener fields on the other bank. A shortened paper strip is used to produce the three goats, and the Troll is an example of combining a symmetrical design with a folded vertical strip. At the end of the story the Troll figure falls open to demonstrate his tumbling action into the river.

PREPARING THE PAPER FOLDS

Cut a large double news sheet in half in the usual way to form a pair of long paper strips and these are used to make both the folds in the story. Both strips need cutting to a modified size as described.

THREE BILLY GOATS GRUFF

Trim off an 8-inch (200-mm.) section from one of the strips to give you a paper piece measuring 12 inches (300 mm.) high by 24 inches (600 mm.) long. Make two folds—one from each end of the strip—so that the folded-down pieces overlap each other exactly as shown in the sketch. If you mark these folding lines at 8-inch (200-mm.) spacings you can be sure the widths will all be the same. Make a further fold from right to left to give you a centre line and then the goats can be marked out. No holding strip is needed across the top of the packet

BILLY GOATS GRUFF AND THE TROLL

Strip measures 32″ x 9″
(800 mm. x 225 mm.)

2nd fold

3rd fold across

4th fold up

1st fold

Strip measures 12″ x 24″
(300 mm. x 600 mm.)

1st fold

2nd fold

3rd fold

Mark and cut out

Mark and cut

Troll

Finger makes the nose

Open to show Trolls falling

because the goats' horns are adequate to support the figures; the chain link pattern at the base ties the three heads firmly together.

THE TROLL

Use the second long strip for this figure but first cut a piece from one of the long edges to bring the sheet size down to 32 inches (800 mm.) long by 9 inches (225 mm.) wide. Fold this strip up from the bottom twice and then make a third fold across the packet as shown. So far, this folding is the same as for making Humpty Dumpty in the first chapter but we now make an extra fourth fold from bottom to top for marking out a design of a symmetrical pattern. The sketch shows how the Troll is pencilled to the *lower* fold-edge so that his eyes are cut to this line. Ears, mouth, nose and feet are all very simple shapes that are easily cut out during the story to give you a surprisingly intricate design from a small amount of cutting when the figure is opened.

PRESENTING THE STORY: WHAT TO SAY AND DO

'The three Billy Goats Gruff were feeling very hungry and they decided to go across the river to where the fields were lush and green. The journey was but a short distance . . . just over the narrow river bridge . . . and they little realised the difficulties they would encounter along the way!'

By cutting the first strip while you make this introduction—there are no special problems since all the cuts, except the eyes, are made from either side of the folded packet. Press open the centre fold when the cutting is completed and show just one goat as you say:

'The little Billy Goat Gruff was the first to go over the bridge . . . here he is . . . trip trapping over the shaky wooden timbers to get to the other side. But half-way over the rickety bridge he was stopped by a strange creature! Let me cut this other folded paper packet and show you how it looked!'

Place the goat figure—still only opened to show one goat—on the table while you trim away the surplus areas to make the Troll. Open the cut figure one fold to show the full face of the Troll and then poke your first finger through the central cut-out to form a long nose for the figure. The sketch shows how this appears to the audience. Lay the Troll down on the table as you continue the tale.

'The Troll had great staring eyes . . . and a nose like a carrot! At first, he wanted to eat up the little goat . . . but the goat told him to wait till his bigger brother came along. Here is the second goat trip trapping over the rickety bridge!'

Open the goat strip one fold and show a pair of Billy Goats Gruff. Explain how the second goat told the Troll to wait for their elder brother to come over the bridge and then open the strip wide to display all three goats.

'The greedy Troll had a great shock when he saw the size of the big Billy Goat Gruff! . . . he had bitten off more than he could chew! . . . because the eldest goat put down his head and charged with his horns! The Troll was butted into the river . . . . and this is how he looked as he tumbled off the bridge and fell into the water with a mighty splash!'

Pick up the Troll and hold him by his heels, then release the strip so that the chain of Trolls falls down. Because of the symmetrical design of the figures their faces appear the right way up down the length of the paper strip. Conclude the story:

'With the Troll vanquished the three Billy Goats Gruff were able to walk across the rickety bridge and eat their fill of the green, green grass!'

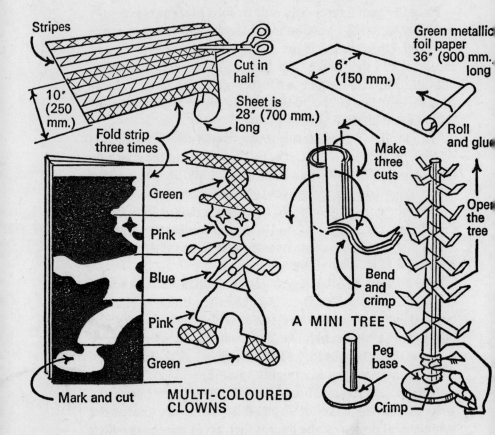

Stripes

10″ (250 mm.)

Fold strip three times

Cut in half

Sheet is 28″ (700 mm.) long

Green metallic foil paper 36″ (900 mm.) long

6″ (150 mm.)

Roll and glue

Make three cuts

Open the tree

Green

Pink

Blue

Pink

Green

Bend and crimp

A MINI TREE

Peg base

Mark and cut

MULTI-COLOURED CLOWNS

Crimp

Festive Paper Cutting

This section of the book describes how the methods and techniques of paper cutting learned in earlier chapters can be used to create some original festive decorations, and the instructions show how all kinds of coloured papers may be effectively employed. Many of the figures in the book lend themselves naturally to seasonal decorations—the skulls and crossbones and the skeletons for instance would be fine for Hallowe'en and could be cut from plain white paper or would give a very shimmery, shaky effect made from silver metallic foil paper. For Easter, Humpty Dumpty would make a fine display in gold foil material accompanied by a strip of Brer Rabbit's Easter bunnies. Christmas is perhaps the most popular time for home decoration and here is a selection of cut paper festoons that are easy to make.

MULTI-COLOURED CLOWNS

Sheets of ordinary gift wrapping papers can be purchased from most stationers and one popular design is printed with a series of coloured stripes. The sheets measure approximately 20 inches (500 mm.) wide by 28 inches (700 mm.) long, so by cutting each sheet down the middle we obtain a pair of long paper strips that only need folding in the usual way. By marking out the clown so that each part of his body coincides with a particular coloured stripe we produce a row of multi-coloured clowns when the cut strip is fully opened. The sketch shows how the figure is divided into sections with the holding strip and hat one colour, the face pink and the jacket and arms blue. The coloured bands repeat in reverse order now giving the row of clowns pink trousers and green boots. Their eyes, mouths and buttons are cut out in the usual way. Several strips of clowns can be glued together to obtain a long festoon for hanging across a wall or window or to make a novel frieze for decorating the edge of a shelf. Other designs in the earlier chapters can be transferred on to the coloured wrapping papers to give you some eye-catching effects.

A MINI TREE

The method of expanding large paper ladders and trees from long strips of paper that have been rolled into tubes can be scaled down to produce miniature Christmas trees. A strip of green metallic foil paper—it is usually green on one side and white on the back—is cut to measure 3 feet (900 mm.) long by 6 inches (150 mm.) wide and is then rolled into a 1-inch (25-mm.) diameter tube and the end lightly glued. It is important to lay the strip down for rolling with the white side uppermost so that the finished tube is green to the outside. Make three cuts—equally spaced round the circumference of the roll—to a depth half-way down the tube—as shown—and then bend the cut sections outwards. Give these sections a little shaping by crimping them over the fingers in the fashion described for the beanstalk construction in an earlier chapter. The mini tree is opened by pulling up the inner coils of the tube until the tree stands about 18 inches (450 mm.) high. A peg base to support the tree is made from a disc of thin plywood 4 inches (100 mm.) in diameter having a wooden dowel that is 4 inches (100 mm.) long pinned and glued to its centre. The base of the tree is placed over the peg and secured by lightly crimping the foil so that it holds firmly to the dowel.

LANTERN FESTOONS

Instead of having to glue sets of four figures together to pro-

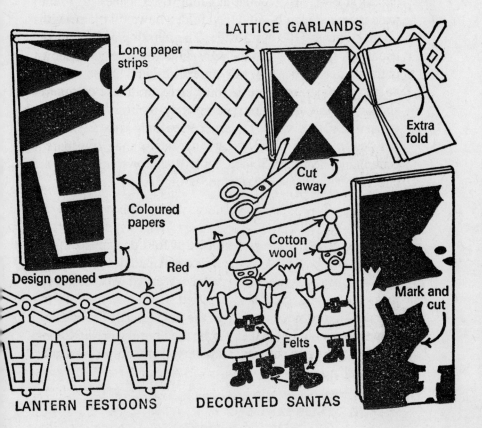

LATTICE GARLANDS

Long paper strips

Coloured papers

Extra fold

Cut away

Design opened

LANTERN FESTOONS

Red

Cotton wool

Felts

Mark and cut

DECORATED SANTAS

duce longer garlands and festoons, strips of wallpaper can be cut to size—6 feet (1800 mm.) long by 9 inches (225 mm.) wide is a good length—and then folded down till the packet is about 4 inches (100 mm.) wide. The marking is done in the usual way by working to the right-hand folded edge as shown in the sketch. Notice how this lantern design is linked together at the top by a decorated holding strip and that two square-shaped windows are cut away completely. If a brightly patterned paper is used the finished lanterns can be hung as cut; by cutting the design out of black paper and then gluing transparent cellophane sheeting behind the lantern windows a most realistic effect is obtained when the festoon is hung across a window.

LATTICE GARLANDS

Long paper strips are given an extra fold bottom to top to prepare the packet for a symmetrical cut design and the sketch shows how the folded paper is marked with a cross for making the interesting lattice design. Cut away the four tri-angular-shaped side pieces, then the strip is ready for opening. Any type of coloured paper can be used but the garlands look very striking when cut from metallic foil and draped vertically on a wall.

DECORATED SANTAS

A very novel and seasonal effect is obtained with this row of decorated Santas which are constructed on a base of red paper. If you use red wrapping paper sheets each sheet can be cut down the middle to make two long paper strips that can later be glued together end to end, once the Santa Claus outline has been cut out. Fold the strips three times and then mark the figures to a centre line on the right-hand fold-edge. A holding strip is needed across the top of the packet and the sketch shows how all the contours round the hat, sack, coat and boots are marked. After cutting out, the strips are laid flat on the table with the red side uppermost, ready for the extra decorations. The cotton wool trimmings are added first and these go on the hat, round the coat cuffs and along the bottom of Santa's coat. If some thin glue is laid on the areas to be treated it is easy to pull out the pieces of cotton wool to the right shape and fix them to the glued places. The eyebrows and beard are also made of cotton wool and the drawing indicates how the beard is shaped with a small hole for the mouth. Santa's belt and boots are cut from black felt and are glued across the waist and over the paper feet. The toy sacks can be covered with brown paper.

STARS AND SNOWFLAKES

Both these designs are developed from square sheets of paper and it does not matter which size you choose because the folding, marking and cutting instructions remain the same whatever the scale. The type of fold employed is fully described in the first chapter for making the Spider in the Tree and uses a square sheet, that can be any size, folded into quarters and then folded twice more, corner to corner, and back to the centre fold as shown in the sketch.

The star design is very easy to mark out using a rule and pencil to draw the two diagonal lines indicated across the triangular-shaped packet. Two straight cuts across these lines produce an eight-pointed star having a smaller star cut out from its middle. If you save the cut-away tip and open it out you will discover a mini-star! Snowflakes are cut from the same type of paper fold to produce the characteristic eight-pointed crystal formation. The sketch shows how to mark the snowflake pattern on the side of the packet, and then the diamonds and pointed contours are cut away cleanly. Use foil glitter paper for both the designs, although larger snowflake patterns intended for window decoration look equally effective when cut from plain white paper.

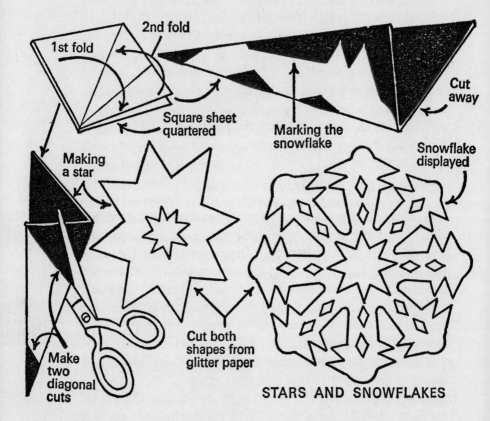

1st fold

2nd fold

Square sheet
quartered

Marking the
snowflake

Cut
away

Making
a star

Snowflake
displayed

Make
two
diagonal
cuts

Cut both
shapes from
glitter paper

STARS AND SNOWFLAKES

Programmes and Presentation

All the stories in the book can be assembled into programmes to make a novel and interesting form of entertainment to suit many occasions. But it is a matter of experience to choose a set of items that will please a particular audience best. Everyone loves to make things and the presenter will find that all audiences will enjoy being shown how to fold, mark and cut the various figures as they listen to the stories. There are many opportunities to present lecture-style demonstrations of the paper cutting art and the author includes some typical examples of programmes that were specially devised for television showings and as lectures.

PROGRAMME NUMBER 1:
A 30-MINUTE SHOW FOR YOUNG CHILDREN

   1. The Pied Piper of Hamelin
   2. Billy Goats Gruff and the Troll
   3. Brer Rabbit
   4. Three Little Pigs
   5. Jack and the Beanstalk
   6. The Magic Kilt

PROGRAMME NUMBER 2:
A 20-MINUTE SHOW FOR OLDER CHILDREN

   1. Going to St. Ives

2. Pirate Treasure with Skulls and crossbones, Padlocks, Swans and Spider in the Tree
3. Jason and the Golden Fleece
4. Siege of the Alamo

PROGRAMME NUMBER 3:
A MIXED AUDIENCE
30 MINUTES

1. Fun at the Fair using the merry-go-round, chain of Humpty Dumptys and the long paper ladder
2. The Pied Piper of Hamelin
3. Brer Rabbit
4. Jason and the Golden Fleece
5. Billy Goats Gruff and the Troll
6. Siege of the Alamo

PROGRAMME NUMBER 4:
5 MINUTES' HIGH-SPEED CUTTING FOR TELEVISION SHOW

1. Production of the long paper ladder
2. Brer Rabbit upside-down figure
3. Multi-coloured Clowns
4. Humpty Dumpty with gold foil paper
5. Giant Beanstalk production: coloured paper

PROGRAMME NUMBER 5:
45 MINUTES' TALK AND DEMONSTRATION

1. Showing how to make all the basic paper folds described in chapter 1, including cutting out all the figures
2. Jason and the Golden Fleece

3. The Magic Kilt
4. Siege of the Alamo
5. Three Little Pigs
6. Festive Paper Cutting showing how to make seasonal decorations from foil and coloured papers